LINA
NILSE.

Progressive
Christians

**DONALD
SCHMIDT**

**A FIVE SESSION
STUDY GUIDE**

Birth OF Jesus

FOR
Progressive
Christians

WOOD LAKE

Editor: Michael Schwartzentruber
Proofreader: Dianne Greenslade
Designer: Robert MacDonald

Library and Archives Canada Cataloguing in Publication
Title: Birth of Jesus for progressive Christians : a five session study guide /
Donald Schmidt.
Names: Schmidt, Donald, 1959- author.
Description: "Bible study." | Includes bibliographical references.
Identifiers: Canadiana (print) 20190138963 | Canadiana (ebook) 20190138971
| ISBN 9781773432878 (softcover) | ISBN 9781773432885 (HTML)
Subjects: LCSH: Infancy narratives (Gospels) | LCSH: Jesus Christ–
Nativity–Biblical teaching. | LCSH: Christmas–Biblical teaching.
Classification: LCC BT315.3 .S36 2019 | DDC 232.92–dc23

Scripture quotations from the *Common English Bible*, copyright © 2011,
Abingdon, Nashville, TN. Used by permission. All rights reserved. Scripture
quotations from *The Message* copyright © by Eugene H. Peterson 1993, 1994,
1995, 1996, 2000, 2001, 2002. Used by permission of NavPress Publishing
Group.

ISBN 978-1-77343-287-8

Published by Wood Lake Publishing Inc.
485 Beaver Lake Road, Kelowna, BC Canada V4V 1S5
www.woodlake.com | 250.766.2778

Wood Lake Publishing acknowledges the financial support of the
Government of Canada. Wood Lake also acknowledges the financial
support of the Province of British Columbia through the Book Publishing Tax
Credit.

Wood Lake Publishing acknowledges that we operate in the unceded
territory of the Syilx/Okanagan People, and we work to support
reconciliation and challenge the legacies of colonialism. The Syilx/Okanagan
territory is a diverse and beautiful landscape of deserts and lakes, alpine
forests and endangered grasslands. We honour the ancestral stewardship of
the Syilx/Okanagan People.

Printed in Canada. Printing 10 9 8 7 6 5 4 3 2 1

CONTENTS

Dedicated to my parents, who taught me to question on my faith journey; and to Kevin, who challenges me always to keep things – even the Bible – as simple as possible.

Thanks

I wish to express utmost thanks to the two groups at First United Church, Kelowna, British Columbia, who engaged this study with me in its early stages and provided valuable feedback. Also, to Mike Schwartzentruber, editor extraordinaire, who helps an author see through their biases with humour, gentleness, and grace; to Robert MacDonald who designed the book and has made it user-friendly; and to everyone at Wood Lake Publishing, who have an amazing desire to serve the progressive church.

For group study

This book is primarily designed to be used in group settings, with minimal instruction for leaders. It is intended to encourage open conversation, for which this study guide is simply that – a guide. When your group gathers each week, you might want to spend a little time at the beginning of the session compiling a list of thoughts, comments, and questions that have arisen for people during the week pertaining to their readings about the birth stories of Jesus. As a group, you can then try to address those questions and concerns during your conversation.

A good facilitator does *not* need to be a biblical scholar of any sort, just someone who can keep the session moving and the conversation on track. Leadership of the group could be held by one person or could change each time, but it is helpful to have a person in charge of the conversation so that the group does not get sidetracked or bogged down.

Spend time with the questions you'll find in the boxes scattered throughout the text; they are designed to provoke reflection. If your group is large – perhaps more than eight to ten people – you might want to divide into smaller groups to discuss the questions and to give people more time to share. But remember, whether you discuss the questions in the larger group or in smaller groups, there are no right or wrong answers. The goal is for group members to exchange thoughts, feelings, and opinions. The point is not to denigrate the stories we already have, but rather to enhance our understanding of them. The exchange of ideas is key to achieving this outcome, which means it's okay for people to disagree. The facilitator should try to hold people's differences of opinion carefully, and to help participants respect each other's views.

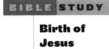

The facilitator will want to review each session ahead of time to get a sense of how much time to allot to the various questions and themes. The amount of time needed will depend on several factors, such as how many people are in the group, their familiarity with scripture, their theological stance, and so on.

For individual study

The best thing is simply to read the study along with a good translation of the Bible – preferably more than one, so you can compare translations. Mark up the study guide with interesting things you learn from other sources, or with questions. Spend time pondering the questions that are listed. You might wish to write comments or answers in the margins, but it's far more important to simply let the questions guide your thinking and reflection.

The video *The Nativity* (produced by Ruth Kenley-Letts; starring Tatiana Maslany and Andrew Buchan; CBC Home Video/Temple Street Productions/Red Planet Pictures/BBC/Entertainment One) can be a helpful addition to this study. Produced in 2010, this portrayal of the nativity differs from others in that it stays very close to the biblical narrative and accurately portrays the social norms of the time as generally understood by modern scholars. There are two items to note, however. First, a shepherd attempts to kill a Roman soldier. While this is not part of the biblical story, the episode illustrates the frustration the Jews would have felt under Roman occupation. The second element concerns the magi, who are portrayed as being three men, two Caucasian and one African. They arrive at the stable the night Jesus is born. Neither of these details is present in either of the stories found in the Bible.

A note on Bible translations

There are many good translations of the Bible. Each has its pros and cons. In this study I include the biblical text for each session, taken either from *The Message* or from *The Common English Bible*. Other modern translations can certainly be used.

What if the Christmas story is not really what many people think it is? What if things happened differently than tradition has maintained over the centuries? What if the biblical account differs – sometimes quite substantially – from the "traditional" account many of us are familiar with from watching or participating in nativity plays? And what if the point the authors of those stories are trying to make is *not* that Jesus was born in a miraculous way, but something that goes much deeper?

The Christmas story most people know comes from pageants, carols, or perhaps a television movie or two. What we recall – and what many people seek to replicate each year – is an odd mixture of the two quite different stories contained in the gospels of Matthew and Luke, with certain pieces almost always present (even though they are *not* in the Bible at all) and with other parts sadly missing. The point of those versions of the story seems to be to nurture some kind of warm, fuzzy feeling that leaves us cooing over a baby, so we can then put the whole thing away as soon as possible after December 25 and get back to life as usual.

That's not what the gospel writers had in mind, however, and neither of them had any interest in giving us a definitive, fact-based story. That was not their issue, and we must not cheapen or lessen the validity of the gospel birth accounts by trying to find factual information in them. For that reason, as well, we need not have difficulty with the fact that there are clearly places where Luke and Matthew appear to contradict each other.

This study is based on the underlying premise that the stories in Matthew and Luke about the birth of Jesus are not literal descriptions of actual events. They are myth in the best and fullest sense of the word, where a "myth," although not literally true, tells the *truth* of things at a much deeper cultural, psychological, or spiritual level.

In other words, Matthew and Luke (and John, which we'll get to in Session 3) each had an agenda. They each wanted to say something about Jesus, to emphasize particular points, and one of the ways they did that was by adding a birth story to their gospels.

This is unusual and important in itself, because people in Jesus' time did not focus on birth stories the way we do today, or at least poor people didn't – and the gospels are set in the context of the poor. Jesus and his family were peasants, and the vast majority of Jesus' early followers were peasants. Very often, children died in infancy, or at a very early age, so concentrating on a birth story was pointless. If a child *did* live beyond infancy, there was usually already another one on the way, and questions about how to feed an expanding family, about how to live from day to day, were far more important than remembering events from the child's birth. (To give a modern example, in Hawaii, people make a bigger fuss over a child's first birthday than they do over the child's birth, because even just one or two generations ago so many children died in infancy that there was no point in celebrating until a child was a year old.)

So what was so important that the writers of Matthew and Luke (and in a very different way the writer of the gospel of John) felt they needed to include a birth story? What was it that they wanted to say?

In his story, Matthew sought to show that Jesus was predestined to rock the boat of the religious establishment even before he was born, and that he was the Jewish Messiah born for all the world – Jew and Gentile alike.

Luke wanted to show that Jesus was predestined to change the world and that he could give Rome a run for its money. He also wanted to emphasize that Jesus was

**Birth of
Jesus**
FOR
Progressive
Christians

Because of the
importance of
Christmas,
how we under-
stand the
stories of
Jesus' birth
matters. What
we think
they're about –
how we hear
them, read
them, inter-
pret them –
matters.
– Marcus Borg
and John
Dominic
Crossan,
*The First
Christmas*

"for" the poorest of the poor, that he was on the side of the "rejects" of the world.

The "birth" narrative in John is very different, and so was his agenda. John wanted to show Jesus as the fulfill-ment of God's cosmic agenda and as having been planned from the very beginning of time.

In this study, then, we are not interested in proving, or even disproving, the historicity of the stories. Instead, our goal is to free ourselves from tradition so we can focus more clearly at what the gospel writers wanted us to see.

■ What happens for you when you hear that the birth narratives might not be "historical" descriptions of actual events?
■ Is the story enriched or diminished for you by focusing on the biblical accounts, as opposed the version we usually hear in nativity plays?

Matthew 1

Let's start with Matthew's gospel. Most scholars think that this gospel was written approximately 80 to 90 years after the birth of Jesus, and some 50 to 60 years after his death – in other words sometime around 80–85 CE. It is therefore extremely doubtful, if not impossible, that the author of this book would have known Jesus directly, although it *is* possible that some of the people he spoke with might have been direct *descendants* of people who had known Jesus personally.

We also don't know who this author was. Tradition says that it was Matthew the tax collector, but there is no reason to believe this, and the Bible itself never even suggests it. We *do* know, however, that the gospel was written for a community of both Jews and Gentiles (non-Jews), and that a central theme in Matthew is that *all* people – Jews and Gentiles alike – can be included in the family of God's people.

Matthew 1:1–17 *(The Message)*
The family tree of Jesus Christ, David's son, Abraham's son:

> *2-6Abraham had Isaac,*
> *Isaac had Jacob,*
> *Jacob had Judah and his brothers,*
> *Judah had Perez and Zerah (the mother was Tamar),*
> *Perez had Hezron,*
> *Hezron had Aram,*
> *Aram had Amminadab,*
> *Amminadab had Nahshon,*
> *Nahshon had Salmon,*

Salmon had Boaz (his mother was Rahab),
Boaz had Obed (Ruth was the mother),
Obed had Jesse,
Jesse had David,
and David became king.
⁶⁻¹¹David had Solomon (Uriah's wife was the mother),
Solomon had Rehoboam,
Rehoboam had Abijah,
Abijah had Asa,
Asa had Jehoshaphat,
Jehoshaphat had Joram,
Joram had Uzziah,
Uzziah had Jotham,
Jotham had Ahaz,
Ahaz had Hezekiah,
Hezekiah had Manasseh,
Manasseh had Amon,
Amon had Josiah,
Josiah had Jehoiachin and his brothers,
and then the people were taken into the
Babylonian exile.
¹²⁻¹⁶When the Babylonian exile ended,
Jeconiah had Shealtiel,
Shealtiel had Zerubbabel,
Zerubbabel had Abiud,
Abiud had Eliakim,
Eliakim had Azor,
Azor had Zadok,
Zadok had Achim,
Achim had Eliud,
Eliud had Eleazar,
Eleazar had Matthan,
Matthan had Jacob,
Jacob had Joseph, Mary's husband,
    the Mary who gave birth to Jesus,
    the Jesus who was called Christ.

¹⁷*There were fourteen generations from Abraham to David, another fourteen from David to the Babylonian exile, and yet another fourteen from the Babylonian exile to Christ.*

As a teenager, I thought I would read the New Testament from cover to cover. It was not a very wise decision, because the New Testament begins with Matthew's gospel, and Matthew's gospel begins with a genealogy, which at first glance is pretty boring. It was only many years later that I discovered great power – and some fascinating messages – hidden in this genealogy. While the genealogy may still seem an odd way to begin the gospel, it is a great way to begin an exploration of the birth of Jesus.

Biblical genealogies have a distinguishing characteristic which is that they generally name only the male side of the lineage.

Read Matthew's genealogy Matthew 1:1–17, above. Don't get hung up on the pronunciation of the names, but notice if there are any you recognize. A few major biblical figures leap out immediately – such as Abraham, Isaac, Jacob, Judah – and then suddenly in verse three we encounter Tamar.

Continue reading and you will find a few other women: Rahab and Ruth (both in verse five); Bathsheba (unnamed, but the "wife of Uriah" referred to in verse six); and finally, in verse 16, Mary.

Let's look at these women briefly. (For a fuller account, you may wish to read their actual stories, referenced and summarized here.)

Tamar (Genesis 38) This is a rather lengthy story in which Tamar is married to Judah's son Er, who dies before they have any children. The custom was for a brother or brother-in-law of the deceased to marry and have a child with the widow. That child would be known as the son

---

BIBLE STUDY

Birth of Jesus
FOR
Progressive Christians

What good is it to me if this eternal birth of the divine Son takes place unceasingly but does not take place within myself?
– Meister Eckhart, *Meditations with Meister Eckhart* **edited by Matthew Fox**

BIBLE STUDY

**Birth of
Jesus**
FOR
Progressive
Christians

or daughter of the deceased husband. In Tamar's case, Er's brother, Onan (Judah's second son), sleeps with Tamar but refuses to impregnate her. According to the story, God punishes Onan with death. After that, Judah refuses to let Shelah, his third and only other son, marry Tamar for fear that if he does Shelah will also die. This leaves Tamar in a desperate position because, having no husband and no child, she is completely without status or means of support within the society of the time. Furthermore, she knows it is not her fault.

Eventually, Tamar disguises herself as a prostitute and Judah (her father-in-law) sleeps with her. Before doing so, however, she extracts some personal items from him as payment. The story would end there except that Tamar becomes pregnant. When Judah finds out that she is pregnant, he is disgraced because he doesn't know the child is his and he assumes that she has bedded a man who is not part of the family or clan – an act punishable by death. He orders her put to death, but Tamar brings out the personal effects he had given her and says, "I'm pregnant by whoever is the owner of these." Judah immediately recognizes that Tamar has been more righteous than he (because he did not fulfill his duty to her by letting her marry Shelah), and all is forgiven.

Rahab (Joshua 2) According to the story, Rahab is a prostitute who shelters some Jewish spies. She hides them in her house, lies to the authorities about their whereabouts, and helps them escape. In return, she and her family are spared when the Israelites enter the land and put everyone else to death.

Ruth (Ruth) Ruth is a foreigner of the tribe of Moab, a group generally despised by the Jews. Her story is often considered to be fanciful, told at a time when Jews were advocating racial purity. The story might therefore have been intended to subvert this "populist" movement, the point being that one of the great ancestors of King David was herself a foreigner. Ruth's husband dies, and she accompanies her mother-in-law, Naomi, back to Bethlehem. Ruth seduces Boaz, a distant relative of Naomi's, who falls in love with her and marries her, thus restoring dignity to Naomi and her family.

> Biblical scholar Edward Campbell Jr. (in *Ruth,* from the Anchor Bible series) has suggested that the story of Ruth was told to illustrate that King David's ancestry was not entirely Jewish. This would have been an important story to tell at times in Jewish history when people were holding others in contempt on religious grounds.
> ■ What might it mean that Matthew has included someone whose story was told to teach people about inclusion?

Bathsheba (2 Samuel 11) David is king over both Judah and Israel, and one day he sees Bathsheba bathing and insists that she be brought to him for sex. She has no say in the matter, despite the fact that she is married, and is sent home afterwards. A problem arises when she learns she is pregnant, and sends word to David. David worries about what to do, and decides to call her husband, Uriah, back from the war where he is fighting in David's army. He sends Uriah home to sleep with his wife – presumably so the pregnancy could be attributed to him – but Uriah refuses to sleep with her while his colleagues are still fighting at the front. David gets him drunk the next night, but still Uriah will not sleep with his wife, so David sends him into the area of heaviest battle and Uriah is killed. David then takes Bathsheba into his home and marries her.

Mary (Matthew 1:16–25; Luke 2:1–20) We'll explore Mary further as we progress through this study, but for now the key point is simply that she is a young girl who becomes pregnant out of wedlock, with the child Jesus. (For background on the use of the word "virgin" in English translations, see box "Matthew's penchant for quoting scripture" on page 22. For background on "Mary's virginity" more generally, see box on page 30.)

■ ■ ■

To give a quick recap of the women mentioned in Matthew's genealogy, we have
■ a woman who disguises herself as a prostitute so that she can have a child by her father-in-law
■ a woman who is a prostitute
■ a woman who seduces a distant relative, again so she can have a child by him
■ a woman who is raped and becomes pregnant, and
■ a young woman who has become pregnant out of wedlock.

In short, there is a sexual aspect to each woman's story. This is not too surprising because in ancient times women were seen primarily as sexual beings. They were also simply chattel, or property. So in addition to their ability to satisfy male sexual desires, their primary worth or value was based on their ability to bear male children in order to ensure that the rest of the husband's property (land and animals and whatever other wealth he may have accumulated) remained in patriarchal line or clan.

We can only speculate as to why Matthew included these women, but perhaps the most likely possibility is that he wanted readers to know, even from the very beginning of his account, that Jesus will be different. Those who might typically be pushed to the side, who might be excluded, who might be rejected, will be included in what is to come and will, in fact, play a pivotal role in shaping the upcoming story. Clearly, the Jesus story is not going to be "business as usual," but will confront many of the mores and traditions of the world and, in so doing, perhaps turn it upside down, or right side up – depending on one's point of view.

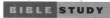
> ■ **What does it mean to you that these women could be seen as "skeletons in the closet"?**
> ■ **Why do *you* think Matthew has included women in his genealogy? What point might Matthew be wanting to make?**

It is also worth noting that the women are Gentiles (foreigners). For Matthew, this was a very important aspect of the ministry of Jesus – that Gentiles as well as Jews would now be included in the family of God's people.

A final piece before leaving the genealogy is simply to note that many scholars recognize that it is difficult to make the historicity of the piece match with other data we have. Matthew offers a very neat – too neat, some say – presentation of three sets of 14 generations. We cannot know with any certainty why Matthew did this, a question that is further complicated by the fact that this genealogy doesn't agree with the one in Luke's gospel.

> ■ **How do you feel about the fact that the genealogy may not be factual?**
> ■ **How important is it to you that the genealogies in Matthew and Luke are not reconcilable?**

We can note, however, that this list includes more than just names, for each name represents a story, and Jesus will become part of those stories. Also, the genealogy establishes the Jewish heritage of Jesus. Because Matthew will take pains throughout his gospel to include Gentiles, it is important for him to begin by demonstrating that Jesus is definitely Jewish.

Matthew 1:18–25*(The Message)*

*18-19*The birth of Jesus took place like this. His mother, Mary, was engaged to be married to Joseph. Before they came to the marriage bed, Joseph discovered she was pregnant. (It was by the Holy Spirit, but he didn't know that.) Joseph, chagrined but noble, determined to take care of things quietly so Mary would not be disgraced.

*20-23*While he was trying to figure a way out, he had a dream. God's angel spoke in the dream: "Joseph, son of David, don't hesitate to get married. Mary's pregnancy is Spirit-conceived. God's Holy Spirit has made her pregnant. She will bring a son to birth, and when she does, you, Joseph, will name him Jesus – 'God saves' – because he will save his people from their sins." This would bring the prophet's embryonic sermon to full term:

Watch for this – a virgin will get pregnant and bear a son;

They will name him Emmanuel (Hebrew for "God is with us").

Then Joseph woke up. He did exactly what God's angel commanded in the dream: He married Mary. But he did not consummate the marriage until she had the baby. He named the baby Jesus.

1:18 Note that there is no annunciation to Mary in Matthew's gospel. We are simply told that she is pregnant by the Holy Spirit. This helps support the understanding that the point of Matthew's story is not the birth

of Jesus, but the visit of the magi (for which we will have to wait until Session 5).

1:19 Joseph is a **"righteous man"** according to the *Common English Bible* and *New Revised Standard Versions* (although *The Message* uses the more ambiguous "noble"). According to the ancient Jewish law (Deuteronomy 22:20–21) Joseph should have Mary killed It seems his conscience won't let him do this, he so chooses to divorce her quietly. Divorce is the only other option because although they are not yet married, they *are* betrothed, and betrothal was a binding contract.

1:20 It is paramount to notice the sequence of events in the story: Joseph is a righteous man; he decides to go against scripture; God then tells him that it's okay, because Mary's child was conceived by the Holy Spirit. It is almost as if Joseph is being rewarded for having chosen to set scripture aside.

> ■ How much of a challenge is it for you to accept that Joseph rejects scripture?
> ■ Why do you think Matthew included a detail like this?
> ■ Why do you think this is often overlooked in the telling of the Christmas story?

1:21 "you, Joseph, will name him Jesus" Jesus is the English transliteration of the Greek transliteration of the Hebrew name Yeshua, or Joshua. This is Jesus' actual name, and it means "God saves."

1:23 Matthew's misuse of the quotation from Isaiah notwithstanding (see box, next page), note that we are told

Matthew's penchant for quoting scripture

Matthew quotes the Hebrew scriptures *a lot*. We might call this practice proof texting, as he takes a snippet here and a snippet there to try to support the story he is telling. This happens in 1:23, 2:6, 2:15, 2:18, and in 2:23. And that's just the birth narrative!

In the context of the birth narrative, Matthew's use of the Hebrew scriptures is problematic in two ways. First, it suggests that the prophet Isaiah predicted the birth of Jesus and the events in his life. We must be careful, however, to note that Matthew does not draw that meaning from the Hebrew text. A modern example might help here.

Several years ago I was at an event where U.S. Congresswoman Shirley Chisholm was the speaker. She declared, "There will be a black president in America soon. If not in my lifetime, then in the lifetime of some who are here today."

Did that mean she was predicting Barack Obama? No. But Barack Obama's election did fulfill her statement.

In a similar way, Matthew's statements from Isaiah may imply to us that Isaiah was talking about Jesus, but that does not mean that Isaiah was doing that, nor that Matthew thought so. Isaiah was speaking about a current situation in his time, not "predicting" the birth of Jesus at all. Matthew is simply pointing out that Jesus fulfilled Isaiah's words.

Second, a huge problem arises when Matthew misquotes the Hebrew scriptures, as he does in verse 23. Isaiah 7:14 states, "Therefore, the Lord will give you a sign. The young woman is pregnant and is about to give birth to a son, and she will name him Immanuel" (*CEB*). Matthew 1:23 quotes Isaiah as, "Look! A virgin will become pregnant and give birth to a son, and they will call him, Emmanuel." Leaving aside the spelling of Immanuel/Emmanuel (which is simply based on how one transliterates the Hebrew), the fact remains that Matthew mistranslates the Hebrew word *almah* (meaning "young woman") as *parthenos*, the Greek word for "virgin." There is little to do but proceed with caution.

the child will be named Yeshua, and then we are given a biblical quote that says his name shall be Emmanuel. An easy explanation is simply that this is a bad edit. Other scholars suggest that Yeshua (Jesus) is the child's name, and Emmanuel is a descriptor, kind of like a title or nickname.

1:25 Matthew tells us that Joseph and Mary do not have sexual relations until after the birth of Jesus. For those who wish to believe that Mary was a perpetual virgin, this is taken to mean that they never had sex. However, the text not only does not say that, it implies (by saying "until after") that they did in fact have sexual relations after the birth of Jesus. This would also make sense, because we are told elsewhere in the gospels that Jesus has siblings.

Closing Thoughts

Matthew presents us with a story that challenges many of our sensibilities. It is as if Matthew is saying, "Hey, world, God is changing things. And it shouldn't really come as a shock because God has been doing things differently for a long, long time. God is about including and welcoming people, not about obeying rules that hurt people, and Jesus is coming to help us grasp all that."

Matthew also presents an odd quandary by presenting, in rapid succession, two very different names for Jesus. Yet there is a great power in each name: Yeshua, or "saviour"; and Emmanuel, or "God with us."

■ What does each name say to you?
■ How do you see Jesus living into each of these names?
■ What other names for Jesus speak to you?

Luke 1

Luke 1:1–4 *(The Message)*

1-4So many others have tried their hand at putting together a story of the wonderful harvest of Scripture and history that took place among us, using reports handed down by the original eyewitnesses who served this Word with their very lives. Since I have investigated all the reports in close detail, starting from the story's beginning, I decided to write it all out for you, most honorable Theophilus, so you can know beyond the shadow of a doubt the reliability of what you were taught.

Like Matthew's gospel, we have no real idea who wrote the gospel of Luke and its companion volume the book of Acts. Someone named Luke figures in several of Paul's letters and it's possible this may be the "Luke" who wrote the gospel, but we do not know that. Tradition holds that Luke was a physician, but this idea is based on little more than the fact that he writes with a lot of detail.

Similarly, we do not know exactly when the book was written, although the best scholarly guess is probably sometime between 60 and 80 CE.

What we *do* know is that the author wants to write a very thorough book that includes lots of information and is grounded in history. These assertions govern how Luke writes.

Luke 1:5–25 *(The Message)*

5-7During the rule of Herod, King of Judea, there was a priest assigned service in the regiment of Abijah. His name was Zachariah. His wife was descended from the daugh-

BIBLE STUDY

**Birth of
Jesus**
FOR
Progressive
Christians

ters of Aaron. Her name was Elizabeth. Together they lived honorably before God, careful in keeping to the ways of the commandments and enjoying a clear conscience before God. But they were childless because Elizabeth could never conceive, and now they were quite old.

⁸⁻¹²It so happened that as Zachariah was carrying out his priestly duties before God, working the shift assigned to his regiment, it came his one turn in life to enter the sanctuary of God and burn incense. The congregation was gathered and praying outside the Temple at the hour of the incense offering. Unannounced, an angel of God appeared just to the right of the altar of incense. Zachariah was paralyzed in fear.

¹³⁻¹⁵But the angel reassured him, "Don't fear, Zachariah. Your prayer has been heard. Elizabeth, your wife, will bear a son by you. You are to name him John. You're going to leap like a gazelle for joy, and not only you – many will delight in his birth. He'll achieve great stature with God.

¹⁵⁻¹⁷"He'll drink neither wine nor beer. He'll be filled with the Holy Spirit from the moment he leaves his mother's womb. He will turn many sons and daughters of Israel back to their God. He will herald God's arrival in the style and strength of Elijah, soften the hearts of parents to children, and kindle devout understanding among hardened skeptics – he'll get the people ready for God."

¹⁸Zachariah said to the angel, "Do you expect me to believe this? I'm an old man and my wife is an old woman."

¹⁹⁻²⁰But the angel said, "I am Gabriel, the sentinel of God, sent especially to bring you this glad news. But because you won't believe me, you'll be unable to say a word until the day of your son's birth. Every word I've spoken to you will come true on time – God's time."

²¹⁻²²Meanwhile, the congregation waiting for Zachariah was getting restless, wondering what was keeping him so long in the sanctuary. When he came out and couldn't

 **STUDY**

**Birth of
Jesus**
FOR
Progressive
Christians

speak, they knew he had seen a vision. He continued speechless and had to use sign language with the people. ²³⁻²⁵When the course of his priestly assignment was completed, he went back home. It wasn't long before his wife, Elizabeth, conceived. She went off by herself for five months, relishing her pregnancy. "So, this is how God acts to remedy my unfortunate condition!" she said.

1:5–7 We are introduced to Zachariah and Elizabeth, an elderly couple, both of priestly families. In verse six we are told they are blameless in God's eyes, which significantly sets up verse seven, where we learn they have no children because Elizabeth was "unable to become pregnant." Although being childless is often presented as a punishment from God, clearly this is not the case here, because they are said to be "blameless."

1:8 Zachariah's division served in the temple twice a year, for a week each time.

1:9 Zachariah is chosen by lot to go into the holy place to burn incense. This is a great honour, often rewarded only once in a person's lifetime.

1:11 An angel appears who is later identified as Gabriel (verse 19). See the box on page 28 to learn more about angels.

1:12 The standard reaction to the presence of a messenger of God is fear; the standard first statement of such messengers is, "Don't be afraid."

1:13 The announcement that the child's name shall be "John" would not have been a surprise, except that, given this is Zachariah's first child, one might have expected

"Zachariah, Jr." John ("Yohanan" in Hebrew) means "Yahweh/God has given grace."

1:17 John's ministry will be similar to that of Elijah: he will go before the Lord (understood later as referring to Jesus) and will turn the hearts of parents (or fathers, but Luke's Greek suggests the more generic "parents") to their children, and the disobedient to thoughts of justice and righteousness. In other words, this prophet's teachings will challenge people to turn their lives around.

> ■ Imagine you are Elizabeth or Zachariah. What feelings might you have had in conjunction with this announcement?
> ■ What do you make of Zachariah being struck dumb? Is this a punishment from God?
> ■ Why might Luke have included this?

1:20 There is some humour in the fact that Zachariah is struck dumb; here he has just been given the most amazing news, and he cannot tell anyone! Luke often inserts bits such as this in his texts.

1:24 Elizabeth stays secluded for the first half of her pregnancy; Jews tended to measure pregnancy as 10 lunar months (280 days). Her choice was not uncommon. If one was going to miscarry, it would generally occur earlier in the pregnancy, suggesting this may have happened to Elizabeth previously.

Luke 1:26–45 (*The Message*)

[26–28] *In the sixth month of Elizabeth's pregnancy, God sent the angel Gabriel to the Galilean village of Nazareth to a virgin engaged to be married to a man descended from David. His name was Joseph, and the virgin's name, Mary.*

Upon entering, Gabriel greeted her:

> *Good morning!*
> *You're beautiful with God's beauty,*
> *Beautiful inside and out!*
> *God be with you.*

29-33 She was thoroughly shaken, wondering what was behind a greeting like that. But the angel assured her, "Mary, you have nothing to fear. God has a surprise for you: You will become pregnant and give birth to a son and call his name Jesus.

> *He will be great,*
> > *be called 'Son of the Highest.'*

Angels

Angels in the Bible have virtually nothing in common with the way angels are usually portrayed in art and in Christmas pageants. For the most part, in the Bible they are male and look like other human beings. Often, they are only distinguishable after the fact. In Genesis, for example, the angels that appear to Abraham and Sarah to announce Sarah's pending pregnancy are thought merely to be human, until their divine pronouncement comes true.

It was only in the second through fourth centuries of the Common Era that angels were assigned to various levels in a hierarchy, such as archangels. We are not told how angels came into being, for they are not mentioned in any of the creation stories in the Hebrew scriptures.

Angels acquired wings in Byzantine art, generally thought to be borrowed from Greek figures such as Victory and Mercury, who had wings. Wings become increasingly manifest in Renaissance art, where angels are often portrayed in long white robes and given gentle,

BIBLE STUDY

**Birth of
Jesus**

FOR
Progressive
Christians

> The Lord God will give him
>> the throne of his father David;
> He will rule Jacob's house forever –
>> no end, ever, to his kingdom."

[34] Mary said to the angel, "But how? I've never slept with a man."

[35] The angel answered,

> "The Holy Spirit will come upon you,
>> the power of the Highest hover over you;
> Therefore, the child you bring to birth
>> will be called Holy, Son of God.

[36-38] "And did you know that your cousin Elizabeth con-

beautiful faces, which over time came to appear quite feminine, giving rise to the modern understanding of angels as female, dressed in white, adorned with wings. Such images are powerful and quite lovely, but they are not biblical.

Luke uses angels to express messages from God; it is an angel who tells Zachariah and Mary about the pending birth of their children (unlike Matthew, who tends to have messages from God come in dreams). Perhaps the best way to think of "angels" in this regard is to think of the feeling one sometimes gets that something is going to happen. Or the inner sense that something needs to be done. Such inner "voices" could well be considered angelic, because they may well come from the divine energy within us and around us. The elevation of angels in art has tended to make us think of them as something very special and worthy of adoration, but not something present in our world, whereas the *biblical* image of an angel is just that – the presence of God being heard and recognized by ordinary people.

ceived a son, old as she is? Everyone called her barren, and here she is six months pregnant! Nothing, you see, is impossible with God."

And Mary said,

> *Yes, I see it all now:*
>> *I'm the Lord's maid, ready to serve.*
> *Let it be with me*
>> *just as you say.*

Then the angel left her.

39–45Mary didn't waste a minute. She got up and traveled to a town in Judah in the hill country, straight to

---

Mary's virginity?

I don't know if actual wars have been fought over this issue, but it can feel as though we have at times come close. As far as biblical interpretation is concerned, there seem to be few issues that divide people quite as much as the issue of Mary's virginity and the whole idea of the virgin birth of Jesus. But does it really matter?

It helps to look at what the biblical record does and *does not* say – and at what tradition has placed upon it with tremendous force.

First, why did it matter to Luke? Probably because he was making parallels between the birth of Jesus and the birth of Caesar Augustus – the latter was said to have been born of a virgin, so it may have been important to show that Jesus was, too.

We know that Mary is young. Given that she is not yet married, she is probably in her early teens – maybe 13 or 14.

According to Luke, she is a virgin when told she will have a child, although interestingly he does not say she is a virgin when Jesus is born. So even if one were to take the story literally, there is nothing in Luke's gospel to disagree with

Zachariah's house, and greeted Elizabeth. When Eliza-
beth heard Mary's greeting, the baby in her womb leaped.
She was filled with the Holy Spirit, and sang out exuber-
antly,

BIBLE STUDY

Birth of
Jesus
FOR
Progressive
Christians

> *"You're so blessed among women,*
> *and the babe in your womb, also blessed!*
> *And why am I so blessed that*
> *the mother of my Lord visits me?*
> *The moment the sound of your*
> *greeting entered my ears,*
> *The babe in my womb*

the possibility that, after the angel informed her she would have a child, she and Joseph had sex.

Similarly, while Matthew states that Mary's pregnancy was "of the Holy Spirit" and that Joseph did not have sex with her, some have pointed out that this does not mean she did not have sex with someone – the theory has come forward that perhaps she was raped. In other words, regardless of how she got pregnant, God's Spirit is upon her, and thus Joseph marries her.

The perpetuation of the idea that Mary was a virgin goes far beyond the biblical narrative and plays into centuries of abuse of women. Despite common "myths," there is no connection between a woman having sex and being "pure," yet we have invented this horrific equation between purity and lack of sexuality. The church has, in many forms, told women that it is their natural role and responsibility to bear children, while at the same time denigrating their sexuality and demanding that they deny it! The tradition forced on Mary is a perfect example of this. Somehow, she is supposed to be both "mother" and "virgin."

skipped like a lamb for sheer joy.
Blessed woman, who believed what God said,
believed every word would come true!

1:26–27 The angel Gabriel reappears when Elizabeth's pregnancy is over halfway through, and informs a "virgin" named Mary that she will have a child. Mary is understandably confused by all this, as she has never had sex with a man before.

> ■ **How important for you is the whole issue of Mary's virginity?**
> ■ **Why do you think Luke tells the story in this way?**
> ■ **Is the idea of the virgin birth an important part of your image of Jesus?**
> ■ **How readily can we grasp the simplicity of what the Bible tells us, when tradition has overshadowed it greatly?**

A woman's position in her husband's family was never secure until she bore a son. Only then did she have a "blood" relationship that secured her place.
– Bruce Malina and Richard Rohrbaugh, *A Social Science Commentary on the Synoptic Gospels*

1:38 Many times, when a Hebrew prophet is called to ministry they quickly make up excuses for why they can't say "yes": Moses points out that he doesn't speak well; Isaiah says he is a man of "unclean lips"; Jeremiah says he is too young. However, Mary – called to a powerful prophetic role as the mother of the Messiah – says "Let it be with me just as you have said." (This caused someone in a Bible study group to remark, "Maybe God should have called more women.")

> ■ **What do you make of Mary's response to the angel?**
> ■ **How would you have answered?**

Mary

BIBLE STUDY

**Birth of
Jesus**
FOR
Progressive
Christians

The Bible does not tell us nearly as much about Mary as tradition has presented to us. (In fact, the Qur'an contains more about Mary than the Bible does.) We are given one verse about her in Matthew's birth narrative, and a substantial portion about her in Luke. She reappears once when Jesus is 12; at the wedding at Cana in John's gospel; in a story where she is called to intervene when people think Jesus is crazy; at the death of Jesus; and lastly, according to Acts 1:14, at the first gathering of the church after the ascension of Jesus.

Despite the few references, the role of Mary cannot be downplayed. She not only gave birth to Jesus, but she raised him – either with or without Joseph. Many of the things Jesus espoused he would presumably have learned at home, from his parents, and Mary would be key in this. Similarly, her role in the second chapter of John, where she appears to force Jesus' hand at the wedding of Cana, can be seen as a pivotal moment in his ministry.

Lastly, when we read the Magnificat (Luke 1:46–55), we realize that Mary was a prophet, for prophets (despite modern notions) do *not* predict the future but rather read the present. They are the editorial writers of their time, carefully observing the world around them and making comment about the direction things are going, or might go, or should go.

■ Who is Mary for you?

■ What do you think of ways in which the church has portrayed her?

■ What do you think Mary contributed to that first meeting of the early church?

1:39 Mary's visit to Elizabeth is undoubtedly inspired by her desire to see if what the angel said about Elizabeth is true. It also provides Mary a safer place to reflect on her own pregnancy, given that Elizabeth is also experiencing an unusual pregnancy. However, we must not let go of the fact that Mary will face horrific shame and public ridicule when it becomes public knowledge that she is pregnant before being married.

1:44 We are told that, at the sound of Mary's greeting, the child in Elizabeth's womb (John) leapt for joy – an intriguing sign that even before being born, John is aware of the presence of Christ.

Luke 1:46–55, The Magnificat *(The Message)*

*46-55And Mary said,
I'm bursting with God-news;
    I'm dancing the song of my Savior God.
God took one good look at me, and look what
happened –
    I'm the most fortunate woman on earth!
What God has done for me will never be forgotten,
    the God whose very name is holy, set apart
    from all others.
His mercy flows in wave after wave
    on those who are in awe before him.
He bared his arm and showed his strength,
    scattered the bluffing braggarts.
He knocked tyrants off their high horses,
    pulled victims out of the mud.
The starving poor sat down to a banquet;
    the callous rich were left out in the cold.
He embraced his chosen child, Israel;
    he remembered and piled on the mercies,
    piled them high.*

It's exactly what he promised,
   beginning with Abraham and right up to now.

BIBLE STUDY

**Birth of
Jesus**
FOR
Progressive
Christians

This amazing poem has been used in numerous ways over the centuries. It is found in the liturgy of many churches; it has been banned at certain times in various countries because it was thought to be subversive; it has inspired numerous hymns; and it has challenged people who might otherwise think of Mary only as a pretty figure in a nativity scene.

Scholar Howard Hageman once described this piece – known as The Magnificat because of its first word in Latin – as being "the gospel in miniature." And William Barclay wrote, in his *Daily Study Bible*, that "There is loveliness in the Magnificat but in that loveliness there is dynamite."

One does wonder, of course, how it got written down, seeing as it is ostensibly spoken by one illiterate woman to another. (Woman were seldom taught to read or write in those days.) Most scholars thus assume that it is the creation of the gospel writer, Luke. However, there is no reason why it could not have been based on Elizabeth's, or Mary's, recollection told to others. In any event, it is a powerful, prophetic piece.

■ **What does the Magnificat say to you?**
■ **Does this change your understanding of Mary?**
■ **Why do you think it seems important for Luke to place this here at this point of the story?**

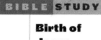

**Birth of
Jesus**
FOR
Progressive
Christians

Luke 1:56–80 *(The Message)*

⁵⁶Mary stayed with Elizabeth for three months and then went back to her own home.

⁵⁷⁻⁵⁸When Elizabeth was full-term in her pregnancy, she bore a son. Her neighbors and relatives, seeing that God had overwhelmed her with mercy, celebrated with her.

⁵⁹⁻⁶⁰On the eighth day, they came to circumcise the child and were calling him Zachariah after his father. But his mother intervened: "No. He is to be called John."

⁶¹⁻⁶²"But," they said, "no one in your family is named that." They used sign language to ask Zachariah what he wanted him named.

⁶³⁻⁶⁴Asking for a tablet, Zachariah wrote, "His name is to be John." That took everyone by surprise. Surprise followed surprise – Zachariah's mouth was now open, his tongue loose, and he was talking, praising God!

⁶⁵⁻⁶⁶A deep, reverential fear settled over the neighborhood, and in all that Judean hill country people talked about nothing else. Everyone who heard about it took it to heart, wondering, "What will become of this child? Clearly, God has his hand in this."

⁶⁷⁻⁷⁹Then Zachariah was filled with the Holy Spirit and prophesied,

Blessed be the Lord, the God of Israel;
*   he came and set his people free.*
He set the power of salvation in the center of our lives,
*   and in the very house of David his servant,*
Just as he promised long ago
*   through the preaching of his holy prophets:*
Deliverance from our enemies
*   and every hateful hand;*
Mercy to our fathers,
*   as he remembers to do what he said he'd do,*
What he swore to our father Abraham –

BIBLE STUDY

**Birth of
Jesus**

FOR
Progressive
Christians

a clean rescue from the enemy camp,

So we can worship him without a care in the world,

made holy before him as long as we live.

And you, my child, "Prophet of the Highest,"

will go ahead of the Master to prepare his ways,

Present the offer of salvation to his people,

the forgiveness of their sins.

Through the heartfelt mercies of our God,

God's Sunrise will break in upon us,

Shining on those in the darkness,

those sitting in the shadow of death,

Then showing us the way, one foot at a time,

down the path of peace.

The child grew up, healthy and spirited. He lived out in the desert until the day he made his prophetic debut in Israel.

1:57–64 Elizabeth has her child and names him John. When Zachariah is consulted he writes down his confirmation: the child shall be named John. At that point, Zachariah can speak again. The fact that the child is named John is a great surprise as everyone would have expected him to be called "Zachariah Junior." Perhaps this is Luke's way of telling us that things are different now that Jesus is on his way.

1:67–80 Zachariah offers a rather lengthy, prophetic poem to his son. It is not surprising that a new parent might have great dreams for their child, but it is intriguing to have such a lengthy piece written down here – there is no other parallel in the New Testament. Zachariah proclaims that, through his child, the people will be rescued from the power of their enemies, and that this child will go before the "Most High" to prepare his way.

BIBLE STUDY

**Birth of
Jesus**
FOR
Progressive
Christians

■ As you read the poem Zachariah spoke, what feelings does it bring to mind for you?
■ Are these the kinds of things you might speak to a child of your own, or to a child in your care?
■ Consider writing a letter or statement similar to this to a child you know. What might you say?

Closing Thoughts

Luke's lengthy first chapter is unique in that it gives us substantial background to the birth of Jesus. Clearly, Luke wants us to know that the birth of Jesus was a planned event, and that it had far-reaching repercussions even before it happened.

Unlike Matthew's gospel, which focused on Jesus' Jewish heritage and the story of Joseph, Luke doesn't mention Joseph at all until chapter 2, and then only incidentally – although also with a sense that we should already know who he is.

■ What does it mean that this story focuses on Jesus' female forebears?
■ Why do you think Luke has emphasized the miraculous nature of the birth of John as well as that of Jesus?
■ Why do you think Luke has placed so much emphasis on Mary and Elizabeth in this first chapter?

Mark and John

BIBLE STUDY

**Birth of
Jesus**
FOR
Progressive
Christians

The Gospel of Mark

At this point, you're probably thinking, "This guy's crazy. There's no Christmas story in Mark's gospel!" You are correct, of course. But that doesn't mean we should ignore this gospel completely as we explore the birth of Jesus. Mark may have things to tell us about this issue, even though he doesn't tell us the story.

In fact, it is intriguing that only two of the gospels offer a narrative story of the birth of Jesus, and they differ; they may not necessarily contradict each other, but they provide us with very different emphases. John's gospel, as we shall see a little later in this session, provides yet another way of looking at the birth of Jesus. But for now, Mark.

Mark's gospel is generally considered by scholars to be the first of the four canonical gospels to have been written, and it is the shortest. Mark's narrative moves at a very quick pace. His constant use of phrases such as "and then" and "immediately" and "the same day" imply that things happened in rapid succession. In fact, all the events of Mark's gospel (after the "40 days" in the wilderness) could have taken place in about a month and a half, which doesn't mean that they actually did happen that swiftly. Also, almost from the very beginning, opposition to Jesus begins to grow. It's as if Jesus' message is so powerful, it is perceived as caustic by those who did not want to hear it, and virtually from the outset they plot to kill him.

Mark 1:1–3 *(Common English Bible)*

The beginning of the good news about Jesus Christ, God's Son, ²happened just as it was written about in the prophecy of Isaiah:

Look, I am sending my messenger before you. He will prepare your way, ³"Prepare the way for the Lord; make his paths straight."

1:1–3 Note how Mark begins his gospel. Scholars tend not to say a lot about the fact that Mark doesn't begin with a birth story, although some point out that historical detail is generally lacking in Mark's gospel anyway. Is the author concerned primarily with Jesus' teachings and not wanting to get bogged down in detail? Were the stories not generally known at Mark's time? Did he simply think it didn't matter? We will never know the answers to these questions.

1:2 "a voice shouting in the wilderness" It is worth noting that in both biblical languages (Hebrew and Greek), the same word is used for both *desert* and *wilderness.* In North America, we might recognize that there is substantial difference between a desert and wilderness, but for the ancient peoples of biblical lands they were essentially the same, especially in one important respect: they were fearful places where life was at risk. Indeed, the Hebrew word for wilderness/desert, *midbar*, comes from a root meaning "far from the voice of God." It is thus interesting that here, in a place far from the voice of God, comes a voice on God's behalf proclaiming to those who live in fear and desolation that there is a new day of hope coming for all people.

 **STUDY**

**Birth of
Jesus**
FOR
Progressive
Christians

■ What does it mean to you that Mark begins his gospel later, with the arrival of John the baptizer – closely followed by the baptism of Jesus – rather than with a birth story?
■ What might Mark be wanting to tell us by leaving out the birth story?

The Gospel of John

John 1:1–5 *(Common English Bible)*

In the beginning was the Word
and the Word was with God
and the Word was God.
²The Word was with God in the beginning.
³Everything came into being through the Word,
and without the Word
nothing came into being.
What came into being
⁴through the Word was life,
and the life was the light for all people.
⁵The light shines in the darkness,
and the darkness doesn't extinguish the light.

Matthew, Mark, and Luke are referred to as the "synoptic gospels" because they present a general overview (a "synopsis") of the life of Jesus, but also because it's as if they tell the story of Jesus through "one eye" or "one lens"; that is, they contain many of the same stories, which convey a very similar "sense" of Jesus, even if they differ in the details. John doesn't do that. Instead, he offers a number of stories that do not exist in other sources: the wedding at Cana, Jesus and Nicodemus, the healing of the man at the pool of Siloam, just to name a few. John also used a great deal of symbolism to make his points – he has Jesus crucified on Thursday, rather than Good Friday, because he wants to express the symbolism that Jesus

was killed the same day that the Passover lambs were sacrificed. While 99.9% of scholars believe this to be historically false, it is a powerful symbol.

The role of symbolism in John's gospel is important for our purposes here because it features a great deal in the piece of the gospel generally known as the "prologue" – chapter 1, verses 1–18.

1:1 "In the beginning" This start to the gospel is not incidental; John seems to want to convey that just as Genesis told of the beginning of time, the arrival of Jesus also signals a new beginning – a new creation.

1:1 "the Word" This is a translation of the Greek word *logos*, which can convey a variety of meanings. Certainly

Very early biblical scholars took great interest in the fact that the biblical creation story in Genesis 1 is similar to the Mesopotamian creation myths. The presence of these similarities reinforced a sense that the stories contained a common truth. However, for modern, more conservative Christian scholars, any similarities between the stories tend to be rejected as fantasy, or as attempts to disprove the biblical stories.

A couple of intriguing contrasts between the two – suggesting that the biblical account may well have been based on other earlier myths, but sought to "correct" them – are that human beings in Genesis 1 appear to be created to *work* with God, rather than to *serve* God. Also, the Mesopotamian concept of *sabbatu* (too similar to the Hebrew *shabbath* – Sabbath – to be ignored) was monthly, but for the Hebrews became a weekly observance, a reminder of God's work in creation.

■ Is your faith enhanced or weakened by recognizing commonalities between the biblical story and other Ancient Near Eastern stories?

■ What might be gained by recognizing similarities?

■ What do you think the purpose of the creation of human beings serves in Genesis 1?

it means more than a printed word on a page. Typically it is associated with the spoken word, even the "Word" in this context is not so much merely spoken as "proclaimed." Most often it is connected to the notion – expressed in Genesis 1 – that God created the universe simply by speaking things into being. It is this Word – this very power and energy – that is now coming into the world.

The Hebrew word used in Genesis 1 is *amar* and its roots, according to the *Theological Dictionary of the Old Testament*, come from a Semitic root meaning "to be bright, to be visible, to make visible, to see, or to inform" (vol. 1, p. 328). This is significant because John will shortly go on to say that the Word is also light for all people. John wants us to understand Jesus as God's Word, and God's light – that is, what God speaks/proclaims, and what makes God manifest.

> ■ How do you understand Jesus as Word?
> ■ How do you understand Jesus as light?
> In his book *Original Blessing*, Matthew Fox translates the Greek *logos* as "Creative Energy" and thus the first few verses of John's gospel would read:
> In the beginning was the Creative Energy:
> The Creative Energy was with God
> and the Creative Energy was God.
> ■ What does it mean to you to understand Jesus as "Creative Energy"?

In the beginning God spoke. This is just like God – part of the way God is. Everything there is comes from God speaking.
– *Good as New: A Radical Retelling of the Scriptures*

1:5 "the darkness doesn't extinguish the light" This is one of the very few places where I like the *King James Version (KJV)*, although for reasons that were never intended. The *KJV* uses a different phrase here: "The light shineth in the darkness, and the darkness comprehended it not." This has become a play on words because of our

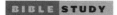 **STUDY**

**Birth of
Jesus**
FOR
Progressive
Christians

shift in how we use the word "comprehend." In 1611 (the year the *KJV* was released), "comprehend" meant to envelop, to overcome – in short, to extinguish by smothering. But over time, the word has changed to take on a meaning of understanding, and thus inadvertently the *KJV* implies that the darkness did not "understand" the light – a fascinating image!

> ■ **What does it mean that the darkness has not overcome/extinguished/comprehended the light?**

John 1:6–8, 15 *(Common English Bible)*
⁶A man named John was sent from God. ⁷He came as a witness to testify concerning the light, so that through him everyone would believe in the light. ⁸He himself wasn't the light, but his mission was to testify concerning the light.

¹⁵John testified about him, crying out, "This is the one of whom I said, 'He who comes after me is greater than me because he existed before me.'"

This text forms a parenthetical piece – or, more precisely, two parenthetical pieces separated by verses 9–14. Many scholars think that they may not have been a part of the original poem. Best guesses are that they were inserted as a way of clarifying that John the baptizer was not *the* light – a way of saying to those who might have thought otherwise, "let's clear this up from the start."

Some scholars believe that John (the gospel writer) may also have been addressing the reality that in the earliest of biblical times, Jesus and John the baptizer had distinct sets of followers and thus were seen as competitors by some. Despite John's fine words at the baptism of

Jesus, he does not stop what he is doing in order to follow Jesus. This possible rivalry only ends with the death of John.

John 1:9–14, 16–18 *(Common English Bible)*

⁹The true light that shines on all people
    was coming into the world.
¹⁰The light was in the world,
    and the world came into being through the light,
    but the world didn't recognize the light.
¹¹The light came to his own people,
    and his own people didn't welcome him.
¹²But those who did welcome him,
    those who believed in his name,
    he authorized to become God's children,
    ¹³born not from blood
nor from human desire or passion,
    but born from God.
¹⁴The Word became flesh
    and made his home among us.
We have seen his glory,
    glory like that of a father's only son,
    full of grace and truth.
¹⁶From his fullness we have all received grace upon grace;
    ¹⁷as the Law was given through Moses,
    so grace and truth came into being through Jesus Christ.
¹⁸No one has ever seen God.
    God the only Son,
    who is at the Father's side,
    has made God known.

Here, the emphasis moves from seeing Christ as the Word, to describing him as the light.

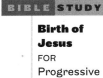

1:10–11 We have to be so very careful not to lapse into anti-Semitism here, because tradition has often – and wrongly – done that. Notice what the text actually says. In verse 10, we are told that "the world" did not recognize the light. Accordingly, the expression "his own people" in verse 11 would more likely mean not "the Jews" (one religion or ethnic group) but rather Christ's own species: God came as a human being, and we (human beings) did not recognize him. If we are to understand "his own people" to mean "the Jews," then verse 12 does not make sense; rather, if this refers only to the Jews rejecting Jesus, presumably verse 11 would say something like "some of his own people (that is, the Jews) didn't believe him, but those who did" were authorized to become God's children. But the text doesn't say that. The implication we are left with is that the world rejected Jesus, but some people (both Jews and Gentiles) did accept him, and they are now God's children.

Law or Way?

The word *Torah* is generally thought to mean "law." But such a translation is neither accurate to the way in which the word was originally used, nor in keeping with a Jewish understanding of the term today. It comes from the root *hari*, which means "to guide or teach." The word has more to do with education than it does with legality; it is more about learning to live as God's people, and far less about rules that must be obeyed, or else.

The problem arose when the Septuagint translation of the Hebrew Bible – done some time in the third century BCE – rendered the word as *nomos* in Greek, which in those days meant "norm, standard, or doctrine." Later the word came to mean "law" in Greek, and that

1:12 "human desire or passion" "Human desire" here would be a reference to the act of sex between people who are in love with each other; "passion" here would refer to casual sex or sex out of wedlock. There is a sense in the Greek that the former is based on romantic feelings and/or mutual respect, while the latter is more a reflection of basic carnal desire (physical gratification). Regardless, the point is clear. No matter how we are conceived, being spoken of here has nothing to do with our human birth, but simply means we are born from God.

1:14 "made his home among us" This expression could also be rendered "he pitched his tent in our midst." This has the wonderful sense of showing that God (present in the world through Christ) is portable, moves where we go, and is present wherever and whenever we need God to be. Given that for the Jews there was a time when they thought God had stayed in Jerusalem while they were

BIBLE STUDY

Birth of Jesus

FOR
Progressive
Christians

meaning became a common understanding (at least by non-Jews) of the word *Torah*.

Perhaps a further piece of irony is that the term is generally applied to the first five books of the Hebrew Bible – Genesis, Exodus, Leviticus, Numbers, and Deuteronomy. While some of these books (such as major portions of Leviticus) are concerned with law, the overall story is about establishing a community, and figuring out our relationship with God. Thus, the word is better understood as "guidance" or "teaching" than "law," at least the way we would use the word "law" today. Many Jews prefer to translate *Torah* into modern English as "the way," which denotes the sense that the *Torah* contains stories to guide us in living God's way. It is undoubtedly not coincidental that the first Christians were called people of "the Way."

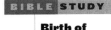

sent off to exile in Babylon, this is very good news. God can be found where and when we need to find God.

> ■ What does the portability of God mean to you?
> ■ What are some of the ways in which you take God with you into your daily living?

1:16 We need to be careful with this verse, as it has often been seen as a rejection of the Torah (often understood as "law" – see box on page 46) that came through Moses. But is it really that, or is it an expansion, perhaps, or a realization that the Torah – the way – is a gift, a joyous thing, and *not* a burden? It is as if John is saying, "God cared for us that way, and now God also cares for us this new way." It's not an "and/or" proposition; it's a "both/and."

1:18 "No one has ever seen God; ... the only Son ... has made God known." This is another way of expressing Matthew's point that Jesus would be known as Emmanuel, meaning "God with us." This adds a very human element to John's gospel. Jesus may be Word and Light and at times indefinable, but he is also the one who has simply come to make God visible to us, in our world. It is we, the followers of Jesus, who are challenged to go the next step and take the message of God's unconditional love – made so very visible in Jesus – into the rest of the world.

Closing Thoughts

The beginning of John's gospel is over-brimming with enthusiasm. It is a little as if someone filled with good news rushes into the room and they can't even spit it out in full sentences because they are so overwhelmed. The news comes in fits and starts, in a rush of exciting bits that can only be put together when the person calms down, catches their breath, and starts at the beginning. What an amazing way to begin the story of Jesus!

■ What might move you to this kind of enthusiasm?
■ What sort of news could overwhelm you?

Luke 2:1-39

The second chapter of the gospel of Luke is the quintessential Christmas story – the one upon which the bulk of Christmas pageants are based, and which has found its way into millions of Christmas cards and works of art. Yet for all of its familiarity we do not know it very well. We think we do, but what we really know is the story that has been passed along through tradition, which has its own flavours quite independent of the biblical narrative. However much we may continue to appreciate the "traditional" story, it is vital to point out that the biblical account is different and, if we are to be biblical Christians, we need to pay a little more attention to the biblical story.

Luke 2:1–7 *(Common English Bible)*
In those days Caesar Augustus declared that everyone throughout the empire should be enrolled in the tax lists. *2This first enrollment occurred when Quirinius governed Syria. 3Everyone went to their own cities to be enrolled. 4Since Joseph belonged to David's house and family line, he went up from the city of Nazareth in Galilee to David's city, called Bethlehem, in Judea. 5He went to be enrolled together with Mary, who was promised to him in marriage and who was pregnant. 6While they were there, the time came for Mary to have her baby. 7She gave birth to her firstborn child, a son, wrapped him snugly, and laid him in a manger, because there was no place for them in the guestroom.*

2:1 While many scholars have played with the Greek text and have twisted and bent and massaged it handsomely in an effort to explain the census to which Luke refers, it is generally assumed that the census simply did not occur. There is no record anywhere – other than in the gospel of Luke – of this census taking place. The only census ever recorded that took place during the reign of Quirinius affected only Judea, and not Galilee, and it took place around 6 or 7 CE. But when or even if it really happened isn't Luke's concern. Luke needed a device to get Joseph and Mary to Bethlehem, and the census seemed a good way to do that.

■ **Does it matter to you if the census never took place?**
■ **What does it do to the story, to realize that it begins with a statement that may not be historically accurate?**

2:1 "throughout the empire" While the Greek *text* refers to the whole world, in New Testament times that simply meant the world that was governed by Rome (that is to say, the Roman Empire).

2:3–4 Given that the census undoubtedly did not happen, the details become moot. However, this story provides Luke with the opportunity to "prove" Joseph's descent from King David.

Son of David

Jesus is often referred to as "son of David" and this has led many to assume that he was descended from King David. Indeed, the genealogies of both Matthew and Luke suggest that this is the case. However, the term "son of David" was also used to refer to someone who modelled behaviour similar to that of David. If someone did a good deed, they were thought to be akin to David, and thus were referred to as a "son" of David.

■ What does it really mean for Jesus to be descended from King David?

■ How important is it for you to think of Jesus as being descended (biologically) from King David?

■ Why do you think Luke wanted to make this connection?

2:5 As so often happens in a story about a pregnant woman, people get uncomfortable with the details, and so they often get confused. It doesn't help that the ancient Greek manuscripts cannot agree here, either.

It is commonly understood that Mary is "betrothed" to Joseph, meaning that she is engaged to be married to him. Such an engagement was binding under Jewish law. Perhaps because it would have been considered scandalous for an unmarried man and woman to travel together, some ancient manuscripts refer to Mary as Joseph's "wife." This has led some scholars to assume that this is more original and that later copies reverted to "betrothed" to preserve Mary's virginity. (Remember, however, that nothing in the story tells us that Mary is still a virgin.) To complicate matters a bit more, some manuscripts have "betrothed wife," which is a conflict in terms! The key in this part of the story is simply to establish that Mary and

Joseph will end up together in Bethlehem, and that she is pregnant.

2:7 This is a difficult verse because so much of the tradition seems to depend on it. In the *King James Version* it reads like this: "And she brought forth her firstborn son, and wrapped him in swaddling clothes, and laid him in a manger; because there was no room for them in the inn."

First, we are sometimes confused by the use of the words "swaddling clothes." This simply refers to cloth wrapped rather tightly around a child, to restrict their movement and keep them warm; a baby blanket works well in our modern world.

Second, there is no small amount of confusion around the word "inn." It conjures up images of a motel, and in fact it seems that several inns have crept into the story in many pageants, with Mary and Joseph going to one inn and then another, only to be turned away and forced into a stable. But you may notice that there is no stable mentioned in this verse at all. And frankly there isn't an "inn" (in the modern sense) either.

The translation of the verse in the *Common English Bible* is more accurate and gives us a clue to what Luke really intended. The Greek word the *King James Version* renders as "inn" is *kataluma*, which refers to the place where guests would sleep – presumably in a house (hence the reference to it as "guestroom" in other translations). Some translations render it as "living space," which is accurate as well. The key point is that *kataluma* does *not* refer to a hotel, or motel, or bed and breakfast. It means that there were already guests staying in the house and, given that Mary and Joseph were not high-ranking, it would not have been odd to put them somewhere else. The modern equivalent might be to say to someone, "Aunt Myrtle is in the guest bedroom so I'll put you on the hide-a-bed in the family room."

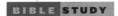

In those days, people often kept animals in the house with them, at least in a room that might also be the sleeping quarters for hired hands, and/or children. Which brings another interesting aspect of the story into the mix. While there are no animals mentioned (despite their appearance in numerous Christmas carols!) there probably *would* have been people there. The idea of no one coming to the aid of an obviously pregnant teenager is at best absurd. And while fathers are frequently present at the birth of their children in our time and place, it would have been completely unheard of for Joseph to attend the birth in Mary and Joseph's time.

The story so far

Let's pause here and catch our breath. In those seven simple verses there is a lot of information – and many parts of the traditional story that are *not* present.

■ How does it feel to confront the biblical story in its incredible simplicity?
■ What does it do to your understanding of Jesus to realize that he may not have been born in a stable? that Mary and Joseph would probably not have been on their own? and that this birth would not have been seen as quite so unusual then as we tend to think of it now?

Luke 2:8–20 *(Common English Bible)*

8Nearby shepherds were living in the fields, guarding their sheep at night. 9The Lord's angel stood before them, the Lord's glory shone around them, and they were terrified.

10The angel said, "Don't be afraid! Look! I bring good news to you – wonderful, joyous news for all people. 11 Your savior is born today in David's city. He is Christ the Lord. 12This is a sign for you: you will find a newborn baby wrapped snugly and lying in a manger." 13Suddenly

BIBLE STUDY

**Birth of
Jesus**
FOR
Progressive
Christians

a great assembly of the heavenly forces was with the angel praising God. They said, ¹⁴"Glory to God in heaven, and on earth peace among those whom he favours."
¹⁵When the angels returned to heaven, the shepherds said to each other, "Let's go right now to Bethlehem and see what's happened. Let's confirm what the Lord has revealed to us." ¹⁶They went quickly and found Mary and Joseph, and the baby lying in the manger. ¹⁷When they saw this, they reported what they had been told about this child. ¹⁸Everyone who heard it was amazed at what the shepherds told them. ¹⁹Mary committed these things to memory and considered them carefully. ²⁰The shepherds returned home, glorifying and praising God for all they had heard and seen. Everything happened just as they had been told.

2:8 Traditionally, we have assumed that Jesus was born at night, although verse eight does not say this exactly – it simply tells us that the angels arrived to tell them the good news during the night. This fulfills a lovely bit from the apocryphal book Wisdom of Solomon: "It was then, while everything was wrapped in a gentle silence, and half a night had already passed, that your all-powerful word had leaped down from heaven, the royal throne" (18:14–15a).

The reference to the shepherds being in the fields all night suggests that Luke intended sometime between May and November, which conveniently (or inconveniently, depending on your point of view) leaves out December 25. This is hardly surprising since the connection of the birth of Jesus with that date did not occur until the fourth century CE.

But from the Christmas text two phrases will not leave you: the heartening "Fear not" and the challenge "to all people."
– Albertine Loomis, *Na Himeni O Ka 'Ekalesia*

December 25

It is not surprising that the actual date of Jesus' birth is not known, and attempts to establish it with any kind of certainty are doomed to failure. People in ancient cultures were simply not concerned with such things, and birthdays were not observed. Indeed, birth stories themselves were rare, which may explain why Matthew and Luke have different versions, and Mark and John include no narrative at all. Matthew and Luke are less concerned with telling us the "facts" around Jesus' birth, and are more concerned with telling us what it *means*.

The celebration of December 25 as Jesus' birthday began with missionaries who went to northern Europe and encountered practices designed to appease the sun, which seemed to disappear on December 21. People were afraid they might have offended the sun god, and that it might not reappear. They brought evergreens into their homes (sound familiar?) and prayed for the sun's return. Christian missionaries lost no time in telling them that they need not fear, because the real light of the world, Jesus the Christ, had been born at this time, and that he was far more important than the sun.

■ Is it a problem for you that Jesus was not born on December 25?

2:9 It helps to remember that biblical angels generally look just like ordinary people, which is why they are seldom recognized (see box on p. 28). What makes the appearance of this angel – and the subsequent company mentioned in verse 13 – special is the fact that God's glory shone around, presumably meaning the night was filled with a bright light. Some have suggested that this could be explained by clouds moving away to uncover a full moon, but one has to wonder if it really matters how it might have occurred, if it occurred at all.

2:10 **"good news to all people"** Some people believe this only refers to "all Jews," given that this is the announcement of the birth of the Jewish Messiah, descended from King David. However, given that Luke is a Gentile and is aware of how the gospel includes people such as him, he may well mean that the angels are announcing news that is quite literally "for *all* people."

2:14 Having just suggested that Luke may have meant this news for all people – Jew and Gentile alike – the expression "peace among those whom God favours" suggests that only *some* people are to be included, or at least only some will reap the benefits (peace) of this birth.

> **The expression "those whom God favours" in verse 14 can seem troubling. However, most scholars assume that it was written by early Christians, a group who were feeling mistreated, and it would have been important to them to declare that only those who please God can in fact receive divine favour.**
> ■ **How does this sit with you?**
> ■ **How might you understand or explain it?**

2:15 The reference that the angels returned to heaven suggests only that they went off into the distance, or disappeared into the dark of the night, not that they had wings.

2:18 **"Everyone who heard it"** This is a clue that there were other people in the room with Mary and Joseph, or

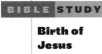
at least close by. Until this point, they would simply be aware that a young woman (Mary) had given birth. Now, with the news the shepherds bring, they are aware that the child is God's intended saviour, and that God is involved in telling the world about him.

2:19 We sometimes gloss over the reference to Mary pondering all of this in her heart, but imagine the situation Luke is trying to paint for his audience: a young girl of about 14 or 15 has just had her first child in a strange place, and some people she doesn't know come and tell her that angels told them about her child's birth. Even if she was already aware that her child was special, this would really bring it home. Surely this young girl must be more than a little overwhelmed.

2:20 This is, according to Luke, the first act of Christian evangelism; the shepherds cannot contain their joy.

Shepherds

While Jesus will be referred to as the good shepherd, the presence of shepherds in the story of his birth probably has more to do with the fact that there were far more sheep than people in Palestine. Shepherds were a dime a dozen, and generally seen as being low class. They worked long and extremely difficult hours, needing to be on alert for predatory animals that would attack the defenceless sheep. They would have spent long nights taking turns staying awake. Yet it is to them that the first announcement of the birth of Christ comes.

Many in Luke's time would have seen shepherds as rough, dishonest, and even outside of the Jewish Law.

■ Why do you think Luke has placed shepherds in his birth story?

■ Whom might they represent today?

■ What might their presence tell us of Jesus' ministry that is to come?

21When eight days had passed, Jesus' parents circumcised him and gave him the name Jesus. This was the name given to him by the angel before he was conceived. 22When the time came for their ritual cleansing, in accordance with the Law from Moses, they brought Jesus up to Jerusalem to present him to the Lord. (23It's written in the Law of the Lord, "Every firstborn male will be dedicated to the Lord.") 24They offered a sacrifice in keeping with what's stated in the Law of the Lord, A pair of turtledoves or two young pigeons.

25A man named Simeon was in Jerusalem. He was righteous and devout. He eagerly anticipated the restoration of Israel, and the Holy Spirit rested on him. 26The Holy Spirit revealed to him that he wouldn't die before he had seen the Lord's Christ. 27Led by the Spirit, he went into the temple area. Meanwhile, Jesus' parents brought the child to the temple so that they could do what was customary under the Law. 28Simeon took Jesus in his arms and praised God. He said,

> *29"Now, master, let your servant go in peace according to your word,*
>> *30 because my eyes have seen your salvation.*
> *31You prepared this salvation in the presence of all peoples.*
> *32It's a light for revelation to the Gentiles and a glory for your people Israel."*

33His father and mother were amazed by what was said about him. 34Simeon blessed them and said to Mary his mother, "This boy is assigned to be the cause of the falling and rising of many in Israel and to be a sign that generates opposition 35so that the inner thoughts of many will be revealed. And a sword will pierce your innermost being too."

36There was also a prophet, Anna the daughter of Phanuel, who belonged to the tribe of Asher. She was very old. After she married, she lived with her husband for seven years. ³⁷She was now an 84-year-old widow. She never left the temple area but worshipped God with fasting and prayer night and day. ³⁸She approached at that very moment and began to praise God and to speak about Jesus to everyone who was looking forward to the redemption of Jerusalem.

³⁹When Mary and Joseph had completed everything required by the Law of the Lord, they returned to their hometown, Nazareth in Galilee.

2:21 "**when eight days had passed**" This is simply the biblical way of saying "a week later." Jesus is circumcised, as would be the case for any Jewish male infant, and named. The name "Jesus," better rendered Yeshua, is the same name as "Joshua," and means "God saves."

2:22 Every woman who gave birth was required to go to the priest to satisfy laws dating to the earliest days of Hebrew society and culture. Many of the ancient laws had to do with "leakages" – that is, any apparent breaches of the bodily system that allowed or caused anything to flow, from a simple cut to menstrual flow, and most certainly the birth of a child. Some scholars think this has more to do with the simple fact that there was great concern that the flow might not stop on its own, and going to the priest was equivalent to a modern trip to the doctor for a checkup.

2:24 The laws of Leviticus required the offering of a year-old lamb. However, provision was made for the poor, who could instead bring a pair of turtledoves or young pigeons. This verse is thus an indication that Mary and Joseph are relatively poor.

Jewish Jesus

This brief story of the circumcision and naming of Jesus, and of the ritual purification of his mother, remind us that Jesus is born into Jewish society. This piece ought never be forgotten, especially in light of anti-Semitism. Jesus was a Jew, and his family were devout Jews. While Jesus appears to expand the understanding of Judaism by inviting into God's family *all* people – not just those racially descended from Abraham and Sarah – Jesus remains a Jew for his entire life.

■ What does it mean to you that Jesus is Jewish?

■ What does it mean to you that his parents observed the intricacies of the law?

2:25–38 In these verses we encounter two prophets, Simeon and Anna, who are both elderly. While we are not given Simeon's actual age, we are told that he had spent his entire life anticipating the birth of the Messiah, and we are told that Anna is 84. This may be a symbolic number, as it is seven (the traditional number for perfection) times 12 (the number of the tribes of ancient Israel). Thus, her age could imply that everything the 12 tribes had longed for is now perfected.

These two prophets could be listed as bit players in the story – they certainly don't figure as significantly as Mary and Joseph, or the shepherds and angels (and seldom get included in any pageants). Yet their role is important, for they give credibility and legitimacy to the identity of Jesus. An old man sees the child and says "now I can die happy, for I've seen God's salvation." An old woman sees the child and has to tell everyone about who he is and who (or what) he will become.

2:39 Almost as a footnote, verse 39 tells us that Mary and Joseph did the things the law required, and then went home, to Nazareth in Galilee. This wouldn't be worth mentioning except that Matthew offers up a quite different story, as we shall see in the last session in this book.

Closing Thoughts

Undoubtedly Luke 2 is the Christmas story with which most of us are most familiar – it is the source of most greeting cards (religious ones anyway) and virtually all pageants. But biblical account is not quite the same as most people's recollection, or as most Christmas pageants.

■ How do you feel about this?
Ultimately, we need to step back and ask ourselves a bigger question.
■ Is the weight and importance of this story in the details, or in the overarching message that Jesus was the embodiment of God's love?
■ Did God "send" Jesus, or did Jesus come into the world like the rest of us, and grow in spiritual maturity and wisdom into the fullest possible expression of divine love?

Matthew 2

In the modern world, we are obsessed with facts. Stories must be "proven to be true" to have much validity. Such, however, was not the case in the ancient world. "Facts" were far more fluid, and symbolism was just as important. That does not mean, of course, that stories rich in symbolism cannot also be factual, but it does remind us that sometimes what appear as facts may not be.

Is this a problem? Absolutely not. The gospel writers want to paint a picture of Jesus, which they do. Whether it is completely "factual" should not matter. I've said this before, but as we approach the second chapter of Matthew it's good thing to remember.

Matthew 2:1–12 *(Common English Bible)*
After Jesus was born in Bethlehem in the territory of Judea during the rule of King Herod, magi came from the east to Jerusalem. ²They asked, "Where is the newborn king of the Jews? We've seen his star in the east, and we've come to honor him."
³When King Herod heard this, he was troubled, and everyone in Jerusalem was troubled with him. ⁴He gathered all the chief priests and the legal experts and asked them where the Christ was to be born. ⁵They said, "In Bethlehem of Judea, for this is what the prophet wrote:

> *⁶You, Bethlehem, land of Judah,*
> > *by no means are you least among the rulers of Judah,*
> > > *because from you will come one*
> > > *who governs,*
> > > *who will shepherd my people Israel."*

Julian wrote out of a long biblical tradition of storytellers who understood, somehow, that mere facts could never contain the wonder they felt in their souls – their intimate experience of God.
– Ralph Milton, *Julian's Cell*

**Birth of
Jesus**
FOR
Progressive
Christians

It came with-
out ribbons! It
came without
tags! It came
without pack-
ages, boxes, or
bags.
– Dr. Seuss,
*How the
Grinch Stole
Christmas*

[7]Then Herod secretly called for the magi and found out from them the time when the star had first appeared. [8]He sent them to Bethlehem, saying, "Go and search carefully for the child. When you've found him, report to me so that I too may go and honor him." [9]When they heard the king, they went; and look, the star they had seen in the east went ahead of them until it stood over the place where the child was. [10]When they saw the star, they were filled with joy. [11]They entered the house and saw the child with Mary his mother. Falling to their knees, they honored him. Then they opened their treasure chests and presented him with gifts of gold, frankincense, and myrrh. [12]Because they were warned in a dream not to return to Herod, they went back to their own country by another route.

Enter the magi. Right off the bat, tradition goes flying. The biblical text never mentions "kings"; we are never told how many there are; they do not have names; they do not represent a variety of nations (thus, there is no reason to think of one of them as black, despite frequent portrayals in nativity scenes); and we do not even know if they were all men.

Magi – the singular is magus – were astrologers. Over the centuries this simple fact made some people squeamish, and so they got elevated to being kings. In an Armenian gospel dating from the sixth century, they were given names and listed as kings of the Hindus, Arabs, and Persians. It was also said that they arrived in Bethlehem with 12,000 soldiers and more than the biblical three gifts, including rare fabrics, ancient writings, cinnamon, silver, sapphires, and pearls. It is a fanciful story to be sure, and yet the idea that these visitors were kings who come from different nations tended to stick.

2:1–2 This is a logical sequence of events. Because they are looking for a king, they naturally would start their search at the royal palace in Jerusalem. They note that they saw a star when they were in the east. (The Greek is a bit ambiguous, but it's the only thing that makes sense as they could hardly have come from west of Jerusalem.)

2:3–6 "Herod...was troubled." Understandable, seeing as these strangers ask for the new "King of the Jews" and he believes *he* is the king of the Jews! He quickly consults his legal experts and they in turn consult the scriptures, finding a verse in Micah that tells us that the Messiah is to be born in Bethlehem.

While the story of the magi is probably made up by Matthew as a way of showing that Gentiles from far and

---

Herod the Great, and Herod Antipas

Herod the Great is an intriguing character. He was born around 72 or 73 BCE, and died in 4 BCE. (This fact is well attested in history, and thus leads to the general conclusion that Jesus was born prior to that date.) Herod is a king, but he must answer to Rome. He has forged a tentative alliance with the Roman Emperor, so long as the Jews are somewhat "obedient" and don't rock the proverbial Roman Imperial boat.

Herod was a tyrant, at various times ordering three of his sons to be killed, one of whom was an infant at the time. This tells us of his paranoia, that he believed his infant son might rise against him. Caesar Augustus, on hearing this story, is said to have remarked, "I'd rather be Herod's pig than his son." It is no surprise, then, that in Matthew's story Herod panicked.

It is worth noting that the Herod who reigns during Jesus' ministry is Herod the Great's son, properly known as Herod Antipas.

■ What might it mean that Jesus is born during the reign of a tyrant?

■ Taking the story metaphorically, what does that tell us of the kind of person Jesus is destined to become?

wide recognized Jesus as a new leader, this episode is based somewhat on the fact that Herod was known for his paranoia.

2:7–10 While the story does not tell it here, the implication is clear that Herod has no intention of worshipping this newborn king, but would like to crush him. He sends the magi on their way, asking them to stop back on their way home.

2:11 This verse is interesting on a couple of counts. First, notice that the magi greet Mary and Jesus in a house, not in a stable. Also, notice that Joseph is not present in the story. This latter fact contributed to the rumour that Joseph must have died when Jesus was young. While this seems likely because he disappears (after Jesus is about 12 in Luke's gospel) there is nothing to suggest that he was substantially older than Mary, something that has been suggested to support the idea that he was impotent

Reading the story metaphorically

The point of the story for Matthew seems clear: the Jewish Messiah being recognized by the wider world. Having established the Jewishness of Jesus, Matthew now gives us a story telling us that foreigners (not Jews) are the first to recognize and worship the Christ. They offer highly symbolic gifts, traditionally taken to mean that Jesus would be a king (gold); a priest (frankincense, used in animal sacrifices to make them smell better); and would die for the people (myrrh, a valuable perfume used in embalming). At the end of the story, the magi go home by a different route; once we encounter Christ, we are called/challenged to live our lives differently, moving in a different direction, and avoiding the evils (represented by Herod) that plague our world.

■ What symbolism(s) do you take from this story?
■ How can it influence your life?

and thus made no sexual demands on her, allowing her to remain a virgin. Of course, given that the gospels tell us Jesus had sisters and brothers, one is left to wonder how this might have worked.

2:12 Verse 12 is significant. The magi go home by a different way, having been warned not to return to Herod.

Matthew 2:13–15 (*Common English Bible*)
13When the magi had departed, an angel from the Lord appeared to Joseph in a dream and said, "Get up. Take the child and his mother and escape to Egypt. Stay there until I tell you, for Herod will soon search for the child in order to kill him." 14Joseph got up and, during the night, took the child and his mother to Egypt. 15He stayed there until Herod died. This fulfilled what the Lord had spoken through the prophet: I have called my son out of Egypt.

This tiny passage presents an intriguing problem, because Luke says the family moved to Nazareth where Jesus grew up, and Matthew says they had to flee to Egypt. Matthew will spend much of his gospel drawing parallels between Jesus and Moses, in an effort to suggest that Jesus is the new Moses. Thus, it's a nice touch to suggest that, like Moses, Jesus comes from the foreign (and exotic, by ancient Hebrew standards) land of Egypt.

■ **How is Jesus like Moses?**

Matthew 2:16–18 (*Common English Bible*)
16When Herod knew the magi had fooled him, he grew very angry. He sent soldiers to kill all the children in Bethlehem and in all the surrounding territory who were two years old and younger, according to the time that he

 **STUDY**

**Birth of
Jesus**
FOR
Progressive
Christians

had learned from the magi. [17]This fulfilled the word spoken through Jeremiah the prophet:

[18]A voice was heard in Ramah,
weeping and much grieving.
Rachel weeping for her children,
and she did not want to be comforted,
because they were no more.

This is a tragic story and there is no way around that. It also probably didn't happen. Josephus, the key Jewish historian of the period, misses few opportunities to point out that Herod was a tyrant, yet he does not mention this story. Nor does anyone else; it is unique to Matthew.

The story has a clear historical parallel, however – the death of the male children at the time of the birth of Moses. In addition, Matthew makes reference to the Exile, the time when the Jews were sent away from the Promised Land. Jeremiah, the great prophet of the Exile, is the source of the quotation in verse 18 about Rachel weeping for her children. It is as if Matthew wants us to grasp that Jesus is not only *similar* to Moses, he is in fact *greater* than Moses, for he "survives" two tyrants, as it were. For Jews of the day, the two lowest points in their history were the time in Egypt that led to the Exodus, and the time of the Exile in Babylon.

> **Matthew wants us to understand that Jesus comes through times of tyranny.**
> ■ **What does that mean to you?**

Matthew 2:19–23 *(Common English Bible)*

[19]After King Herod died, an angel from the Lord appeared in a dream to Joseph in Egypt. [20]"Get up," the angel said, "and take the child and his mother and go to the land of Israel. Those who were trying to kill the child are dead."

²¹Joseph got up, took the child and his mother, and went to the land of Israel. ²²But when he heard that Archelaus ruled over Judea in place of his father Herod, Joseph was afraid to go there. Having been warned in a dream, he went to the area of Galilee. ²³He settled in a city called Nazareth so that what was spoken through the prophets might be fulfilled: He will be called a Nazarene.

Now, at long last, the holy family goes to Nazareth. Just as in the beginning of Matthew's story of the birth of Jesus, events are guided by the dreams Joseph has. And for Matthew the point of it all seems to be so that Jesus will be called a Nazarene.

Why?

We don't know for sure. However, Matthew uses the form of the word Nazorean rather than the more familiar Nazarene to describe Jesus. This may be Matthew's way of drawing a link to a Nazirite, who was someone set apart for the service of God. Thus, Matthew may be wanting to make this final point in the Christmas story, that this Jesus we have been reading about is set apart for the service of God. Yes, he is the Jewish Messiah. And, Matthew hastens to add, he is also recognized by Gentiles, and he is set apart to serve God. For Matthew, writing in turn for a church that is seeking to be Christian, while being occasionally torn apart by the struggle between being Jewish or Gentile, this is important. *Serving God is what matters, not our heritage.*

Closing Thoughts

Each of the gospels tells us something about the birth of Jesus.

For Matthew, Jesus came for Jews and Gentiles, survives tyrants and historical tragedies, and is going to turn the world upside down and right side up.

For Mark, the birth of Jesus doesn't matter because it is the gospel he proclaimed that really matters.

Birth of Jesus
FOR
Progressive
Christians

A simple Jesus

When I led this study at First United Church in Kelowna, British Columbia, in the fall of 2018, one of the participants frequently struggled with the study, as her approach came from a stance of seeing Jesus – and other biblical characters – as being ordinary people, and thus the miraculous nature of some of the stories left her struggling. She offered this insight:

Jesus came into the world in a normal way. He was conceived in a normal manner and was born a normal way. His upbringing was normal. He was just a normal guy – just like you or me. That's what's amazing. Jesus was like any of us. Jesus had some special talents – able to talk to a crowd and a great speaker. But...all of us have special talents. All of us do amazing things. Jesus was special because he recognized his talents and used them. Imagine if we all did that...

For Luke, the birth of Jesus happened in real history, was pre-planned by God, there was great preparation, and when the upper (read: proper) members of society would not make space, others (e.g. shepherds) stepped up and made him welcome.

For John, the arrival of Jesus is cosmic and amazing, and transforms the world from the outset. John's gospel also presents a unique parallel to Genesis because in Christ God is doing nothing less than creating a new universe.

■ Which story do you like best?
■ If you could write your own story, picking and choosing various bits that seem intriguing, what might it contain?

And þay anon knewen hor Lorde

I couldn't resist offering a few additional pieces because, well, they're such fun. This first one is a Bible story, as written down and published in the late 14th century in England. It was written by an Augustinian monk, John Mirk, who was the Abbot of a monastery in Lilleshall. This story, along with many others, was copied by hand and distributed in book form all over England. After the printing press came to England in 1454, Mirk's homilies continued to be published for another 135 years.

Note: The letter þ is called a "thorn" and is pronounced like the "th" in "they" and "there." The letter ȝ is called a "yogh" (yo) and was often used where modern English uses "gh" as in "midnight." The yogh is pronounced like a rough "kt."

And þay anon knewen hor Lorde

But when þay comen ynto þe cyte, hit was soo full of pepull, þat þay myȝt gete hom no herber; but turnet ynto a caue þat was bytwene two howsys, þeras men setten hor capuls when þay comen to þe marked, and fonden þer a crache wyth hay, and setten þe ox and þe asse erto. Pen, a lytyl byfor mydnyȝt, our lady bade Ioseph gete hyr mydwyues, for scho shuld be delyuerd. But, whyle he was yn þe towne aftyr mydwyues, our lady was delyuerd, and lappyd hyr sonne yn clopes, and layde him yn the crache befor þe ox and þe asse. And þay anon knewen hor Lorde, and fellen down on knees, and worschepe hym, and ete no more of þe hay.

Translation: But when they came to the city, it was so full of people that they could find no shelter for themselves, but turned into a cave that was between two

houses, where people put their cattle when they came to the market, and there they found a crèche with hay and they put the ox and the ass there. Then, a little before midnight, our Lady asked Joseph to get midwives for her, because her baby was to be born. But, while he was in the town looking for the midwives, our Lady was delivered, and wrapped her son in cloth, and laid him in the crèche before the ox and the ass. Immediately, they knew their Lord, and fell down on their knees and worshipped him, and ate no more of the hay.

John Mirk [Johannes Mirkus], Mirk's Festial: A Collection of Homilies. *Edited by Theodor Erbe for the Early English Text Society. London: Kegan Paul, 1905, pp. 22–23. English translation by Ann Bemrose.*

This is a most intriguing story, as it suggests that midwives were called (although they did not arrive on time) and that the animals recognized the Christ and worshipped him. Beyond that, it has a very folksy, simple nature to it.

■ What do you take from this story?

The Cherry Tree Carol

This English carol is known to have been sung as early as the 15th century. It is listed as number 54 in the collection of old ballads compiled by American Francis James Child in the 19th century, and has been recorded by a number of artists, notably Joan Baez; and Peter, Paul, and Mary.

The carol tells a tale about the early life of Mary and Joseph. The couple are out for a walk, and presumably Joseph is not yet aware of Mary's pregnancy. If he is, he has chosen to remain quiet about it, even though he knows the child is not his.

When Mary asks Joseph for some cherries, he angrily says, "Why don't you ask the baby's father?" The as-yet-unborn Jesus then commands the trees to bow down and offer Mary some cherries, and they comply. Joseph presumably repents, as he then asks baby Jesus when he will be born, and he offers the date of January 5. This may seem an odd date, but it is the traditional English "Twelfth Night."

Joseph was an old man, an old man was he,
When he married Virgin Mary, the Queen of Galilee.

As Mary and Joseph were walking one day
To an orchard of cherry trees they happened to stray.

Then Mary said to Joseph, so meek and so mild,
"Pick me some cherries, Joseph, for I am with child."

Then Joseph flew angry, so angry flew he,
"Let the father of your baby gather cherries for thee."

Then up spoke Lord Jesus from in his mother's womb,
"Bow low down, cherry trees, bow down to the ground."

And the cherry trees bowed down, bowed low to the
     ground,
And Mary gathered cherries while Joseph stood round.

Then Joseph he kneeled down and a question gave he,
"Come tell me, pretty baby, when your birthday shall be."

"On the fifth day of January my birthday shall be,
And the stars in the heaven shall all bow down to me."

■ Do you think about Mary and Joseph's relationship prior
to the birth of Jesus?
■ What might it have been like?

I Wonder as I Wander

While the author of this hymn is often listed as "anonymous" or "traditional Appalachian," it was largely written by John Jacob Niles, incorporating a fragment (sources disagree as to whether it was one, two, or three lines long) from a young girl called Annie Morgan. The song was first performed in 1933.

The tune that Niles composed is haunting, perhaps contributing to the song's popularity over the years. Of interest is the sense, from the beginning, that Jesus came "for to die." Additionally, the use of the word "ornery" (sometimes spelled orn'ry) is intriguing. While originating in the word "ordinary," it has come to mean "argumentative" or "bad-tempered," which leads many people (for better or worse) to find themselves included in the hymn. The final stanza's suggestion that Jesus could have anything he wanted because "he was the king" is an odd and indirect way of acknowledging Christ's identity, and the reference in the second stanza to "wise men, and farmers, and shepherds, and all" emphasizes that Christ has come for all people.

I wonder as I wander out under the sky,
how Jesus the Savior did come for to die.
For poor orn'ry people like you and like I...
I wonder as I wander out under the sky.

When Mary birthed Jesus 'twas in a cow's stall,
with wise men and farmers and shepherds and all.
But high from God's heaven a star's light did fall,
and the promise of ages it then did recall.

**Birth of
Jesus**
FOR
Progressive
Christians

If Jesus had wanted for any wee thing,
a star in the sky, or a bird on the wing,
or all of God's angels in heav'n for to sing,
he surely could have it, 'cause he was the King.

- For whom do you believe Jesus was born?
- For what purpose(s) was Jesus born?

BIBLIOGRAPHY

Barclay, William. *The Daily Study Bible – Luke.* Toronto: G.R. Welch, 1975.

Borg, Marcus and John Dominic Crossan. *The First Christmas – What the Gospels Really Teach About Jesus's Birth.* San Francisco: Harper, 2009.

Botterweck, G. Johannes and Helmer Ringgren. *Theological Dictionary of the Old Testament – Volume 1.* Trans. by John T. Willis. Grand Rapids: Eerdman's, 1974.

Brown, Raymond E. *The Birth of the Messiah: A Commentary on the Infancy Narratives in the Gospels of Matthew and Luke.* New York: Doubleday/Anchor, 1999.

Fox, Matthew. *Original Blessing: a Primer in Creation Spirituality.* Santa Fe: Bear and Company, 1986.

Long, Thomas G. *Matthew.* Louisville: Westminster John Knox, 1997.

Poston, Elizabeth. *Penguin Book of Christmas Carols.* New York: Penguin, 1987.

Wright, N. T. *John for Everyone.* Louisville: Westminster John Knox, 2004.

Revelation
for Progressive Christians

A SEVEN SESSION STUDY GUIDE

Donald Schmidt

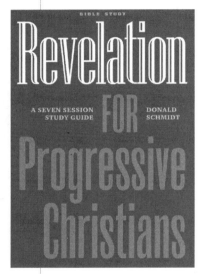

More material has probably been written about the biblical book of Revelation than the rest of the Bible combined – or at least it can seem that way. What's more, people who write or talk about Revelation often have a passion that defies all logic. They speak vividly and forcefully about plagues, and judgements, and the end of the world. All interesting themes – but are they the real concern or message of Revelation?

Revelation for Progressive Christians is a seven-session study guide that invites readers to explore Revelation as a fun, hope-filled book that contains a lot of fanciful imagery and symbolic references, to be sure, but that, at its core, offers words of assurance and hope to the church and its people today.

ISBN 978-1-77343-150-5
5.5" x 8" | 100 pp | paperback | $14.95

Passion & Peace
The Poetry of Uplift
for All Occasions

Compiled by Diane Tucker

All cultures we know of, at all times, have had poetry of one sort or another – chants, songs, lullabies, epics, blessings, farewells – to mark life's most important moments, transitions, and transformations. Ever since our species began using words, we have arranged them to please, to experience the pleasures, the fun, of rhythm and rhymn, repetition and pattern.

Passion & Peace: The Poetry of Uplift for All Occasions was compiled to speak directly to this deep human need, with 120 of the best poems from almost as many classical and contemporary poets. The book also includes a handy thematic index.

A welcome addition to any library and the perfect gift for any occasion, *Passion & Peace* is a heartwarming, uplifting, and inspirational volume.

ISBN 978-1-77343-028-7
6" x 9" | 304 pp | paperback | $24.95

WOOD LAKE

Imagining, living, and telling the faith story.

WOOD LAKE IS THE FAITH STORY COMPANY.

It has told
- the story of the seasons of the earth, the people of God, and the place and purpose of faith in the world;
- the story of the faith journey, from birth to death;
- the story of Jesus and the churches that carry his message.

Wood Lake has been telling stories for more than 35 years. During that time, it has given form and substance to the words, songs, pictures, and ideas of hundreds of storytellers.

Those stories have taken a multitude of forms – parables, poems, drawings, prayers, epiphanies, songs, books, paintings, hymns, curricula – all driven by a common mission of serving those on the faith journey.

Wood Lake Publishing Inc.

485 Beaver Lake Road
Kelowna, BC, Canada V4V 1S5
250.766.2778

www.woodlake.com